Mary Cohen's
Tuneful introduction to 2nd finger spacing

Easy well-known pieces for violin

FABER *ff* MUSIC

CONTENTS

© 1998 by Faber Music Ltd
First published in 1998 by Faber Music Ltd
3 Queen Square London WC1N 3AU
Cover design by S & M Tucker
Illustrations by Todd O'Neill
Music processed by Stephen Keeley
Printed in England by Halstan and Co Ltd
All rights reserved

ISBN 0 571 51806 0

To buy Faber Music publications or to find out about the full range of titles available
please contact your local music retailer or Faber Music sales enquiries:

E-mail:sales@fabermusic.co.uk
Website://www.fabermusic.co.uk

To the teacher

Mary Cohen's Tuneful Introduction to 2nd finger spacing is designed for pupils at a level of about grade one. Its main aim is to reinforce the skill of changing from finger pattern one (FP1: 0 1 23 4) to finger pattern two (FP2: 0 12 3 4).

On pages 4-17 you will find simple well-known tunes, using finger pattern one in a low octave on the left-hand page; on the right-hand page, the same tune is written one octave higher using finger pattern two. Pupils are encouraged to use their aural recognition of the tune to help them play both versions equally well. They may also fill in the star charts which will help with note naming. Further musical interest is added through the 'sound effects files'. These offer opportunities for improvisation and imaginative use of dynamics. Pages 18-23 introduce the sound of a minor 3rd and encourage pupils to transpose and finish off tunes by ear.

When pupils can play all the material in this book confidently, they will be ready to tackle the concepts of scales and keys in *Scaley Monsters*.

Mary Cohen's Tuneful Introduction to 2nd finger spacing and *Scaley Monsters* can be used to supplement the *Superstart* series.

To the pupil

Welcome to the world of the aliens!

FP1 will guide you through the tunes which use finger pattern one (that's when the 2nd finger is close to the 3rd finger).

FP2 will show you how to play the same tunes using finger pattern two (when the 2nd finger is close to the 1st finger).

As you go through the book you can map out the notes on the star charts. Try out ideas from the 'sound effects files' and make up some of your own too. You will probably recognise most of the tunes, which will make them easier to learn. They don't need accompaniments, but one of the challenges on page 24 will help you turn some of them into duets that you can play with your teacher or friends.

*Have fun exploring your violin with **FP1** and **FP2**!*

What shall we do with the drunken sailor?

(lower octave)

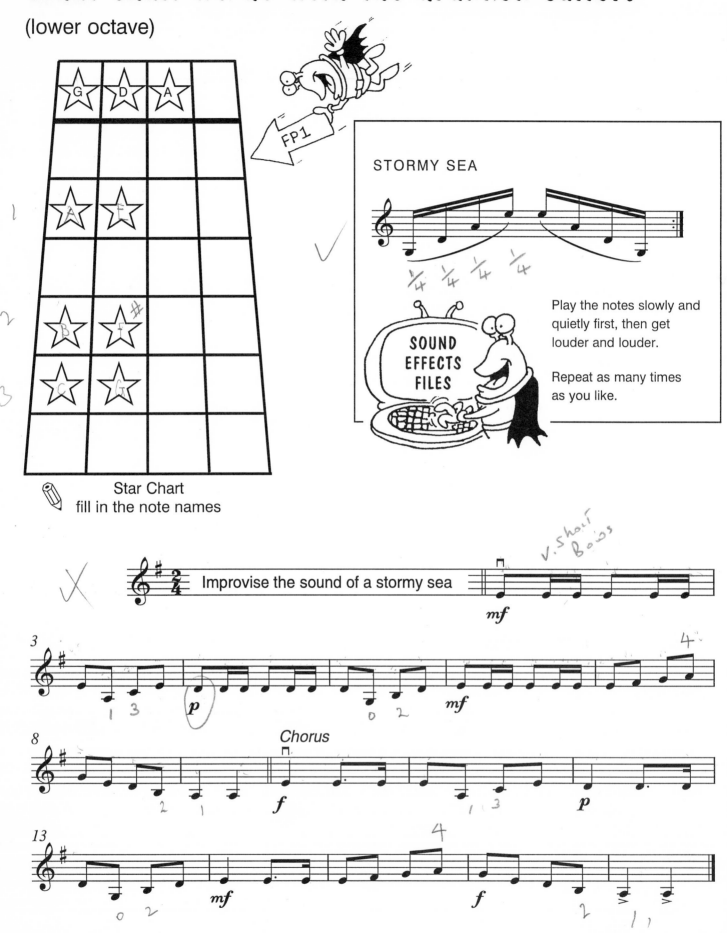

STORMY SEA

Play the notes slowly and quietly first, then get louder and louder.

Repeat as many times as you like.

SOUND EFFECTS FILES

Star Chart
fill in the note names

Improvise the sound of a stormy sea

Chorus

What shall we do with the drunken sailor?

(higher octave)

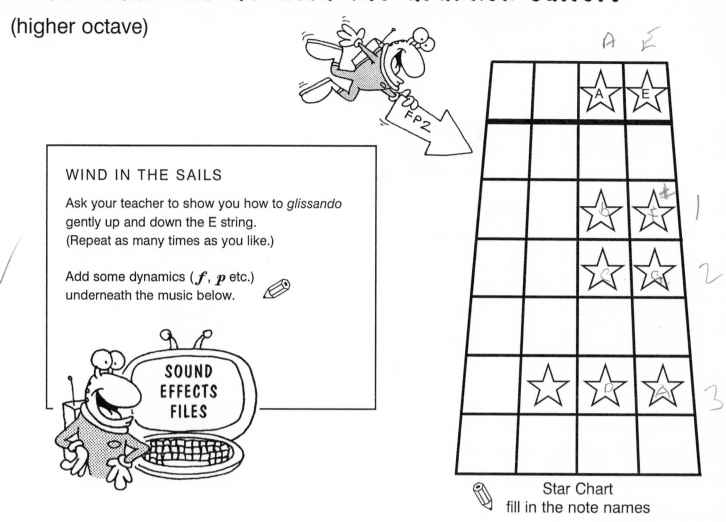

WIND IN THE SAILS

Ask your teacher to show you how to *glissando*
gently up and down the E string.
(Repeat as many times as you like.)

Add some dynamics (*f* , *p* etc.)
underneath the music below.

SOUND
EFFECTS
FILES

Star Chart
fill in the note names

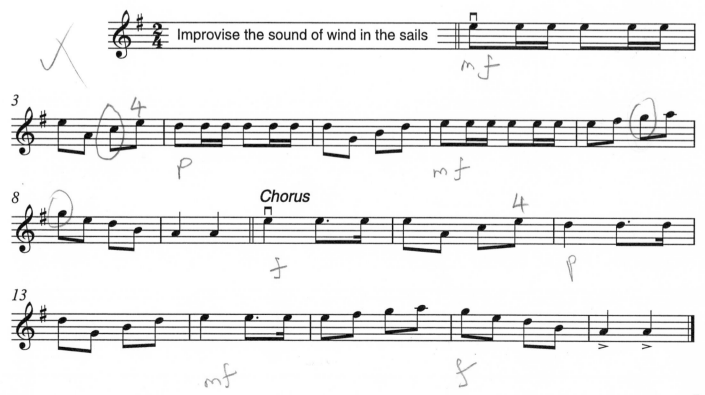

Improvise the sound of wind in the sails

Chorus

Hickory Dickory Dock (lower octave)

Star Chart
fill in the note names

⟋ Click your tongue.

∤ ∤ Say "tick tock" with strong "ck" sounds.

pizz. (pizzicato) – pluck the string.

SOUND EFFECTS FILES

⌢ = pause

tick   tock   tick   tock   tick   tock   tick   tock

tick

tick   tock   *mf*

pizz.

Hickory Dickory Dock (higher octave)

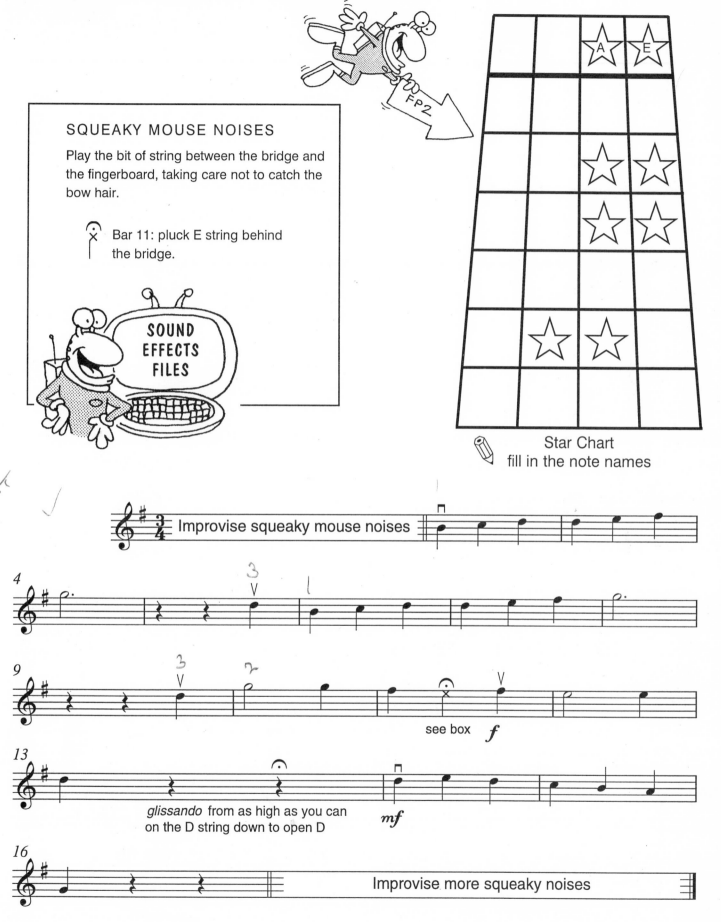

SQUEAKY MOUSE NOISES

Play the bit of string between the bridge and the fingerboard, taking care not to catch the bow hair.

Bar 11: pluck E string behind the bridge.

SOUND EFFECTS FILES

Star Chart
fill in the note names

Improvise squeaky mouse noises

see box f

glissando from as high as you can on the D string down to open D

mf

Improvise more squeaky noises

Three blind mice (lower octave)

Star Chart
fill in the note names

A whole bar rest – do not play, but prepare your bow for the next bar.

$pp < ff > pp$

Start very quietly, get louder and louder, then quieter and quieter.

SOUND EFFECTS FILES

Improvise squeaky mouse noises

Three blind mice (higher octave)

Whole bar rest – this time improvise *eaky squeaky* noises with your mouth.

Choose your own dynamics and write them under the music below.

SOUND EFFECTS FILES

Star Chart
fill in the note names

German folksong (lower octave)

Star Chart
fill in the note names

stamp stamp – try to use one foot then the other.

molto dim. (molto diminuendo) – get a lot quieter.

SOUND EFFECTS FILES

German folksong (higher octave)

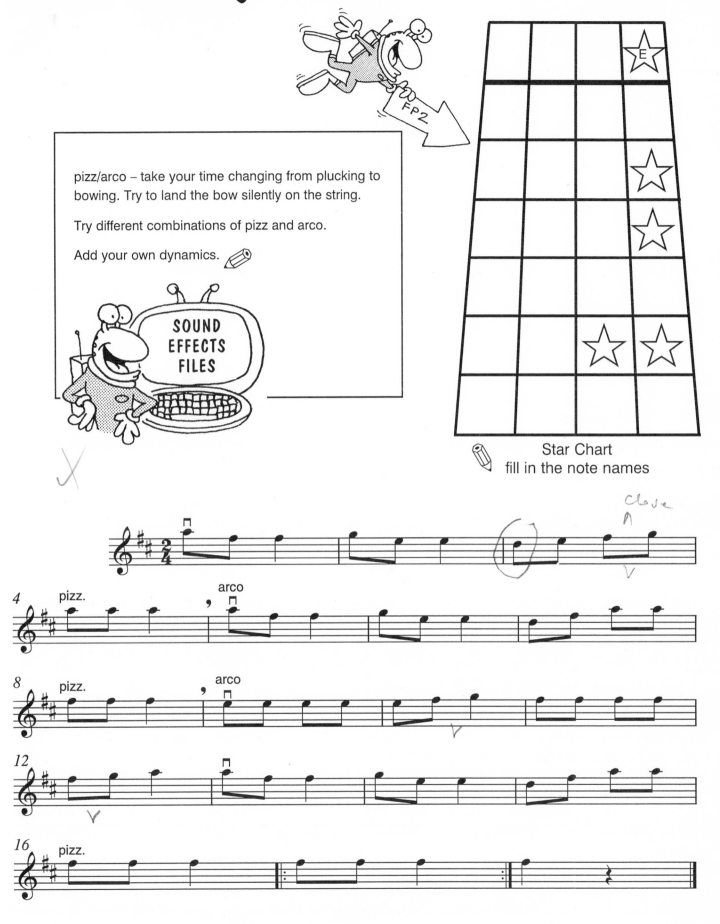

pizz/arco – take your time changing from plucking to bowing. Try to land the bow silently on the string.

Try different combinations of pizz and arco.

Add your own dynamics.

SOUND EFFECTS FILES

Star Chart
fill in the note names

Au clair de la lune (lower octave)

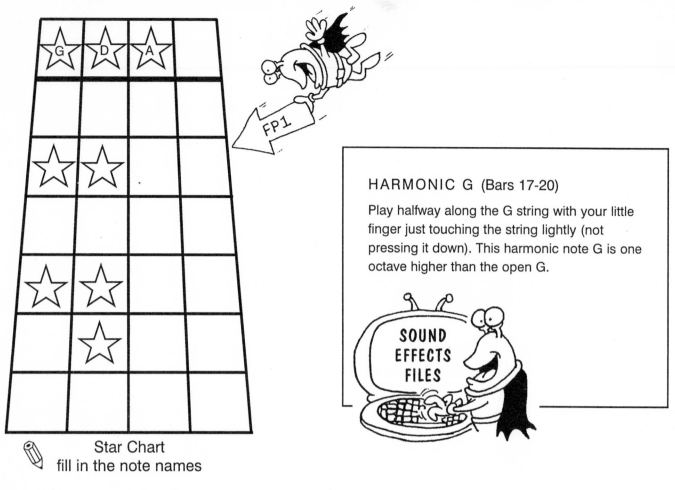

Star Chart
fill in the note names

HARMONIC G (Bars 17-20)

Play halfway along the G string with your little finger just touching the string lightly (not pressing it down). This harmonic note G is one octave higher than the open G.

SOUND EFFECTS FILES

Au clair de la lune (higher octave)

pp *tremolo* (bars 17-18) – a fast, shimmering bow effect; ask your teacher to show you how to play this with a relaxed bow hold.

Add your own dynamics to the rest of the piece.

SOUND EFFECTS FILES

Star Chart
fill in the note names

tremolo near point

pizz.

pp

Oh, when the saints (lower octave)

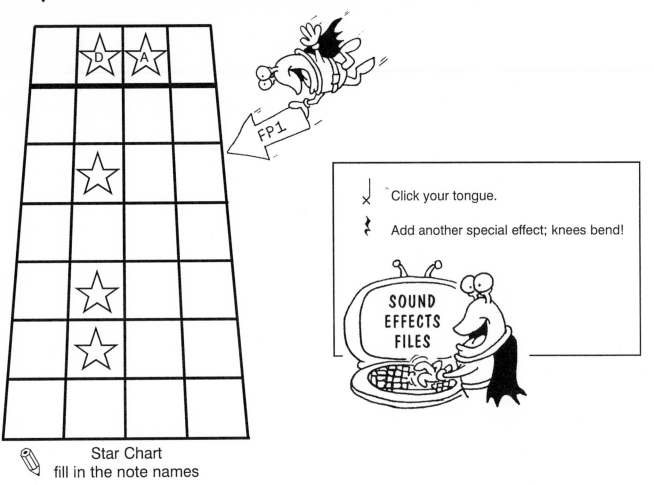

Star Chart
fill in the note names

SOUND EFFECTS FILES

✗ Click your tongue.

𝄽 Add another special effect; knees bend!

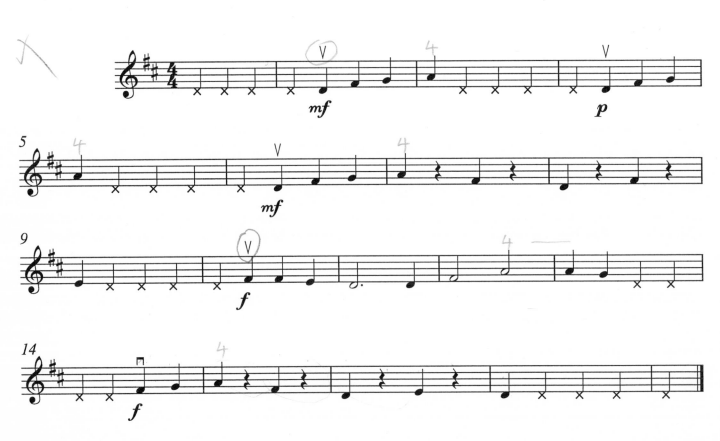

Oh, when the saints (higher octave)

Create your own sound effects and special effects, and add some dynamics.

Star Chart
fill in the note names

Jingle bells (lower octave)

Star Chart
fill in the note names

Bars 1-2, 19-22

col legno – bounce the wood of the bow gently against the string.

SOUND EFFECTS FILES

Jingle bells (higher octave)

Bars 1-2, 19-22

✗ Tap screw end of bow gently against music stand.

SOUND EFFECTS FILES

Star Chart
fill in the note names

arco
mf

5

3 = 3

9

14
f

18

Hot cross buns (major key version)

Star Chart
fill in the note names

Cold cross buns (minor key version)

Star Chart
fill in the note names

Finish by ear

Finish the tune by ear, then decide whether it is FP1 major or FP2 minor.

FP_ m_ _ or

FP_ m_ _ or

FP_ m_ _ or

FP_ m_ _ or

FP_ m_ _ or

FP_ m_ _ or

Merrily we roll along (major key version)

Star Chart
fill in the note names

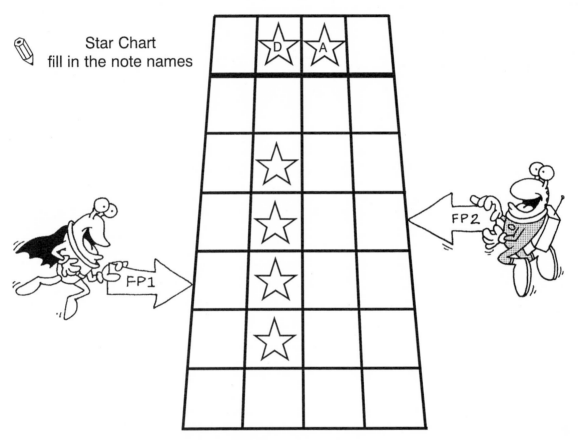

Wearily we crawl along (minor key version)

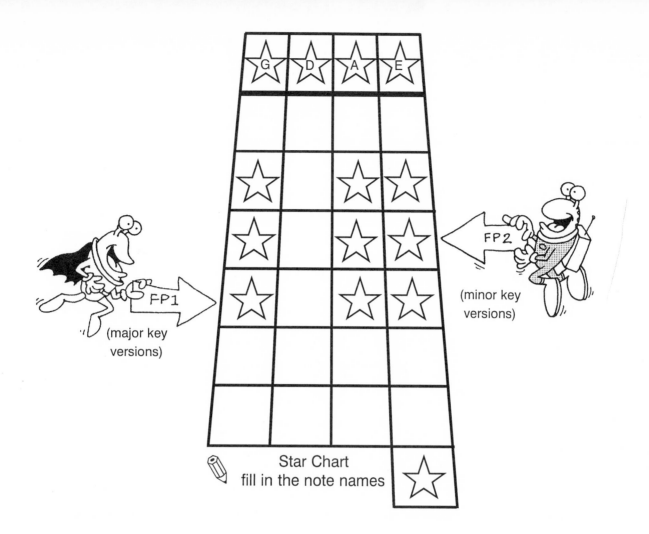

Star Chart
fill in the note names

(major key versions)

FP1

(minor key versions)

FP2

Finish by ear

Finish the tune by ear, then decide whether it is FP1 major or FP2 minor.

FP_ m_ _ or

FP_ m_ _ or

FP_ m_ _ or

FP_ m_ _ or

FP_ m_ _ or

FP_ m_ _ or

One man went to mow (major key version)

Star Chart
fill in the note names

FP1

FP2

VAROOM!!
VAROOM!!

No man went to mow (minor key version)

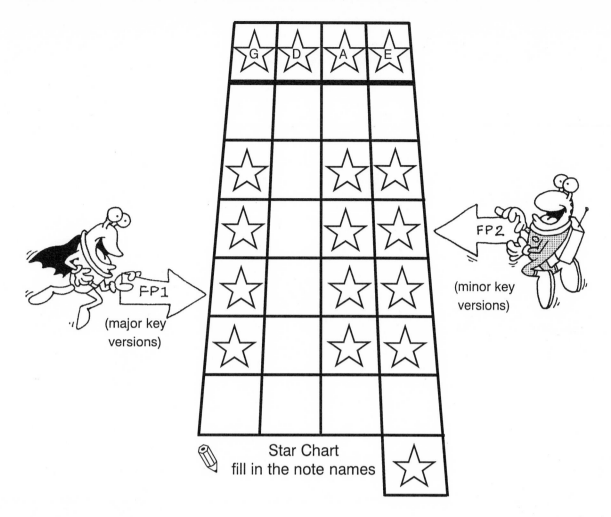

Star Chart
fill in the note names

Finish by ear

Finish the tune by ear, then decide whether it is FP1 major or FP2 minor.

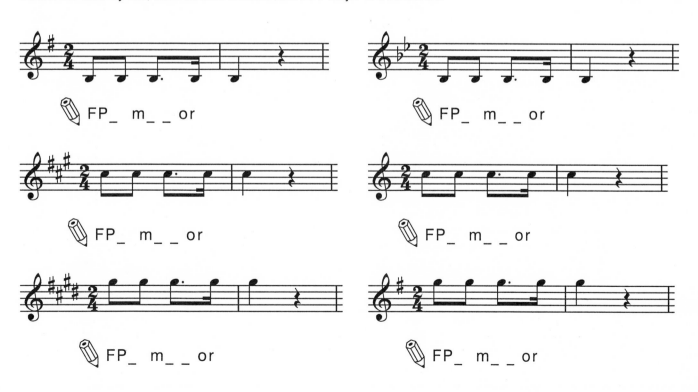

FP_ m_ _ or

FP_ m_ _ or

FP_ m_ _ or

FP_ m_ _ or

FP_ m_ _ or

FP_ m_ _ or

The aliens set seven great challenges from their music explorer's file

 _sk your teacher to play one of the tunes from pages 4-17 in the lower octave while you play the same tune in the higher octave.

 _ow one of the tunes from pages 4-17 in the lower octave while your teacher plays the higher version *pizzicato*.

 _an you turn the Bs on page 12 into B♭s to make it a cloudy night? (Listen out for the moon peeping through the clouds in the middle.)

 _o you know the names of the notes your 2nd finger plays in finger pattern one? And what does your 2nd finger play in finger pattern two?

 _xperiment with the notes played by the 2nd finger in **German folksong** and decide if you like the tune in:
- a major key
- a minor key
- a mixture of major and minor

 _ind and play a tune from another book which uses some finger pattern two notes.

 _ive a concert of your favourite tunes from this book.